A LETTER
TO MY FRESHMAN SELF

SECOND EDITION

A LETTER
TO MY FRESHMAN SELF

SECOND EDITION

A LETTER TO MY FRESHMAN SELF
Second Edition

Copyright © 2018 by Corby Publishing

10 9 8 7 6 5 4 3 2 1

ISBN 978-1-7321150-0-2

Published by
Corby Books
A Division of Corby Publishing LP
P.O. Box 93
Notre Dame, Indiana 46556

Manufactured in the United States of America

PREFACE

I vividly remember the first time I set foot on Notre Dame's campus. My family and I had come out to visit my brother Hunter ('17) for the USC vs. Notre Dame game—and I couldn't stop smiling. The ground was covered in myriad colors of fall leaves and I was proudly wearing my Notre Dame knit hat. It was during that short weekend that I fell in love with Notre Dame. Later on, that spring, I accepted the offer to participate in the Notre Dame Gateway Program. While it was difficult to accept that I would not have the typical college freshman experience, it was worth it because attending Notre Dame was my dream. Looking back I realize that, by making this decision, I chose to surround myself with a group of humble, hardworking, and kind people who would challenge me to grow exponentially. That year, I was determined to make the most of every moment. I didn't want to look back on my four years of college as a senior and find them full of opportunities that I had missed and regretted passing up. My hope is that this anthology of letters written by Notre Dame alumni and students—ranging from the class of 1953 to the class of 2020—will impart insightful advice that will challenge, motivate, and inspire future students to make the most of their time at Notre Dame.

To Elizabeth Boyle, our Editorial Board Director, I offer my greatest appreciation. Thank you for the countless hours you dedicated to transforming our book into a cohesive masterpiece. To Matthew Bulgarelli, our Editorial Board Associate, thank you for your eagerness to help with every step along the way. Your enthusiasm and hard work made this project run smoothly. I am honored to have worked with both of you. Also, my thanks go to Kelsey Allen for designing the cover of this book. I am truly awed by your beautiful interpretation of the Notre Dame Reflecting Pool.

I would like to thank Dean Hugh R. Page Jr. and Assistant Dean Maureen Dawson for their invaluable contributions, guidance, and support for weaving this book into the first-year experience. To Jim Langford, our publisher, thank you for your encouragement and insight. It was an absolute pleasure to work with you. To our mentor and friend, Lily Kang, you are a true gift and thank you for being there to help us throughout the entire process. Words cannot express how grateful we are for the resources, contacts, and wisdom that you imparted to us. Thank you for designing this inspiring project and pushing us all to examine our time at Notre Dame in a deeper, more grateful way. On behalf of the Editorial Board, it was an honor to carry on your legacy.

We would also like to thank the Sorin Scholars Program through the Center for Undergraduate Scholarly Engagement at the University of Notre Dame for their continued support of this project. Additionally we would like to extend our gratitude to the Class Council, Alumni Association, and all academic departments that helped shape this project.

A final thank you goes to all of the Domers, both current students and alumni, who have chosen to contribute to this second edition. I believe that your words of wisdom will inspire the next generation of Notre Dame students to persevere when times get tough, to strive for academic excellence, to foster deep authentic relationships, and to use their talents to make the world a better place.

Love thee, Notre Dame,

Haley Kempf

Haley Kempf
Class of 2020

FOREWORD

As a first-year student walking onto the campus of what was at that time Hampton Institute (now Hampton University) in 1973, I recall feeling more than a little trepidation. I was barely seventeen, naïve, and incredibly shy. Am I ready? Is this the right place for me? Will I make new friends? Can I handle the academic challenges ahead? These were just a few of the questions swirling in my mind. Nonetheless, I was also excited to begin a new adventure away from home and it didn't take long for me to realize that there was something truly inspiring about this time of transition and uncertainty.

However, the breadth, depth, texture, and nuance of that experience have taken me many years to appreciate truly. With the benefit of hindsight, I realize what I might have done differently—perhaps better—to explore, to cultivate a deeper sense of wonder, to master foundational learning principles, and to understand what it meant at that time to be an African American male beginning his education at a historically Black college in the South just five years after the world-changing events of 1968. If I were aware in a visceral sense then of what I now know, I suspect that the itinerary for, and way stations on, my metaphorical first-year journey might have changed significantly.

Having served as Dean of our First Year of Studies for

more than a decade, I now appreciate the importance that the beginning of my own college sojourn—and indeed the first two semesters of any collegiate experience—occupy in the *longue durée* of the quest for an undergraduate degree and a life well lived. The same is true for the contributors to this volume, all of whom have agreed to reach across time and offer constructive advice to their "first-year" Notre Dame "selves." In each of these letters you will find a remarkable mélange of the particular and the universal. A compendium of this kind opens a window onto the world of undergraduate life seen in parallax—one perspective focused on the past, and another on the present. Such a juxtaposition is vital for this work's authors and potential readers insofar as a way is made for both contemplation about the nature of the timeless and more dynamic dimensions of the first-year experience and meaningful conversation among those who have lived it, are in the midst of it, or serve as its stewards. Reflected herein is also the perspectival diversity of a community at once shaped by the values and ideals of the Congregation of Holy Cross' distinctive charism and animated by the hopes and dreams of the faculty, staff, students, and alumni/ae who are part of it.

I commend the editors for their vision, energy, and commitment to this project and congratulate them for bringing it to fruition in record time. My hope is that future first-year students will find in this anthology wisdom and sustenance for the remarkable pilgrimage that is theirs to undertake.

(The Rev. Canon) Hugh R. Page, Jr., DMin, PhD
Vice President, Associate Provost, and Dean – First Year of Studies
University of Notre Dame

TABLE OF CONTENTS

Notre Dame is not a final destination

Dear Freshman Self,

It has been a long time—40 years!—since we have seen one another. I envy your energy and excitement about life, but I have learned a bit in the intervening decades and want to offer a few words of advice as you begin your career at a great University.

First, during your time at Notre Dame, ask big questions—whether or not they are on your class syllabi. Yes, you are busy, but you are unlikely to have the time and environment ever again in your life to grapple with questions about God, what makes a good life, and what your particular calling is. The answers you find to these questions—or your refusal to engage them—will shape the rest of your life.

Second, don't be afraid to make mistakes. You were admitted to Notre Dame because you are talented and accomplished (though, I admit, the class of 1976 is not quite as talented as the class of 2019, 2020 or 2021 will be). You should strive for excellence. But don't let an excessive concern about blemishes on your record lead you to avoid risks. Failures—whether academic, professional, personal, or of any other kind—are painful, but they teach us the most. When I am sizing up a person for a position now, I want to know where they failed and how she or he responded. That teaches me most about who that person is.

Third, come to know the joy of service and the joy of community. I've had the chance to meet many people and have consistently been struck by the irony that the most generous are the happiest. As I look back on the past forty years, the genuine joy I have found in my life is proportional to the degree I have been able to give. It really is true that it is in giving that you receive.

Fourth, make room in your life for silence. Spend time at the Grotto or in your dorm chapel; walk around the lake; take a contemplative walk through the art gallery. You, in 1972, are fortunate not to have the cell phones that seem to intrude so regularly in the lives of students in 2018, but you still need to find time for quiet.

Fifth, cultivate a genuine faith. You will struggle with doubts and questions, but that is all part of developing a true faith. Blasé Pascal said that in faith there is enough light for those who want to believe and enough shadow to blind those who don't. That is why it is faith. I have found that it is precisely struggling through the doubts and questions that has deepened my faith. In moments of darkness and doubt, pray for faith. Make time for prayerful silence in your life.

Sixth, love Notre Dame, but remain eager to get out in the world. After a lifetime of being associated with the University and ten years as its president, I continue to be impressed at the depth of affection students and alumni have for Notre Dame. Yet I'm even more impressed by the good these alumni are doing in the world personally and professionally. Notre Dame is not a final destination, but a place to prepare you to lead, inspire, serve, and better the world.

A few last things: avoid paisley shirts, bell-bottom pants and sideburns. They seem cool now, but your future self will be embarrassed if you are photographed in them. You have two near-contemporaries named Bill Gates and Steve Jobs who will do a lot of talking about something called a "personal computer." Buy stock in their companies. Finally, attend the Notre Dame-UCLA basketball game in 1974. It will be interesting.

From an older, and hopefully wiser, you,

Fr. John Jenkins, C.S.C.

Rev. John Jenkins, C.S.C. '76
Bachelor of Arts in Philosophy

Elected in 2005 as the University of Notre Dame's 17th president, Rev. John I. Jenkins, C.S.C., has devoted himself to fostering the University's unique place in academia, the Church, our nation and the world. A philosopher trained in theology and a member of Notre Dame's Department of Philosophy since 1990, Fr. Jenkins earned undergraduate and advanced degrees from Notre Dame, a doctorate of philosophy from Oxford University, and a master of divinity and licentiate in sacred theology from the Jesuit School of Theology.

Don't compare yourself to others

Mike,

Something you're not very good at is treasuring the last moments of things, so as I write this I want you to calm down and appreciate spending time with your family and relax on your last vacation before you go off to college. Appreciate having your twin brother, Tom, around because I can't really explain to you what that feels like not having him. Appreciate him while he's there and make a good effort to keep in contact often.

Also, you need to be mentally prepared to be lonely, because everyone tells you how you are going to meet a bunch of new people, but no one really explains that it's a process. Understand that there are going to be other lonely people in college. Just because everyone else around you looks like they are happier than you doesn't mean that it is true, and comparing yourself to other people is unhelpful.

You should not compare your college friends to your high school friends, because they are not going to live up to those expectations. This is not because your college friends aren't good people, but they aren't supposed to fill the roles other people had in your life. It's going to be hard, sorting through all the people you meet, to try and find some good

4

friends, but remember not to take everyone at face value either. I know the first time you're going to meet some people in your section, you're going to think they are weird and try to avoid them, but don't. Little do you know that they will become your closest friends in a couple of months.

Don't expect Notre Dame to be perfect. You will have to work harder than you ever have. In a few short weeks, you will decide to join rowing on a whim and that will be the most physically demanding thing you have ever done. Living away from home is something you have never experienced before, and it's not really something you can relate to. You need to realize that Mom, Dad, Amy, Tom, Dan, Maggie, Grandma and Grandpa, and everyone else will not live so close to you anymore. In a lot of ways, it's going to feel like you against the world, as you try and battle school, making friends, keeping friends, time management, and rowing. This might seem intimidating, and it should; college is not a cakewalk. However, you will survive your first semester and do well in a lot of ways, but you need to be prepared for the work and the bad times, because, college is nothing like anything you've ever experienced before.

Sincerely,

Mike

Michael Seraphin '20
Bachelor of Science in Biochemistry and Theology

Michael Seraphin grew up in St. Charles, Illinois, one of the many suburbs of Chicago. He is one of five kids and has a twin brother who attends school at Benedictine College in Atchison, Kansas. He is majoring in biochemistry and theology with the intent of attending medical school. At Notre Dame, he is an active member of the men's rowing team as well as a Compass leader and an Eucharistic Minister for his dorm.

Embrace what
differentiates you from others

Dear Diane,

You chose "Some men see things as they are and say, why?; I dream things that never were and say, why not?" as the theme of your high school graduation speech. This will become the anthem for your bright creativity and will be a guidepost throughout your life. You don't yet see that your uniqueness is an incredible asset, because you might feel that this impedes you from fitting in with the mainstream. Celebrate and nurture this strength for it truly differentiates you in the business world.

Growing is painful. The borders of your world to-date have been narrow. Not everyone has the same benefit you do in experiencing a broader world, and they may not appreciate or may be fearful that you are growing into a new person as a result. It will be OK to leave some of those relationships behind if they no longer align with your broader perspective, although it will hurt to move forward. Unfortunately, not all friendships or relationships last a lifetime. But family does; it is not OK to leave them behind. The good thing is that family is forgiving—especially when you eventually realize they are a pretty awesome bunch.

There is a lot in this world you still don't know. The

older I get, the more I understand how little I will ever know! Seek out the strength and input of those around you, as the result is so much greater than what you alone can do. I know you want to prove your independence and value, but life is a team adventure, not an individual competition.

Learn and practice the art of networking now. Be intentional about your connections in this incredible network of the ND community, which will open many doors for you. Your opportunities will be even more plentiful if you learn to actively foster this gift, as well as the networks from your graduate school and future employers.

Your future is limitless, and you have incredible potential. You are only limited by your self-doubt. Affirm to yourself that you have talents, gifts, intellect and energy— and remember to thank God and your parents for them. But also know that this life isn't just about getting ahead or achieving a goal. You will spend far too many years pouring energy into your ventures, only to realize that just the experience of life offers a much better reward than the taste of success. Yes, it's important to have an eye on the path to the future. The future is long, and interesting, and elusive. But relishing the here and now is what makes your heart smile. Now is real. {Spoiler alert: Hiking through a jungle, riding in a helicopter, landing on a volcano are all way more fun than getting a promotion, a big title, or a raise! And you will experience all these things.}

Work hard, play harder, and have a great life,

Diane

Diane Schwarz '85
Bachelor of Science in Mechanical Engineering
and Bachelor of Arts in English

Diane also has an MBA from the University of Chicago and a flourishing career in technology, with a current role as Chief Information Officer. She lives in Texas with her husband and has two sons. Her volunteer focus is on fostering the STEM community, and she makes as much time as she can to go to concerts and experience new adventures across the world.

Give of yourself

Dear Christina,

The best four years of your life await you. This time at Notre Dame will go by quickly, but somehow 20 years later it will feel like it was just yesterday. You will meet your best friends. You will find yourself. Both will happen, even without you looking. You will carry this time with you for the rest of your life.

Sleep less. Say "yes" more. Repeat those words to remind yourself often. As much as I know now that sleep deeply restores the mind and body (and you will learn to live with less sleep when you have the big family you always dreamed of), try to figure out a way that you are less tied to what you should do and more committed to what you want to do. These memories will last a lifetime, make as many as you can!

Explore. Try new things—join clubs you are interested in even if your friends aren't; or take an elective that you are curious about but scared to try. Love your close circle of friends, but know that having different groups of friends will bring new connections for everyone. Grab a meal with your project teammates. Say yes to attend the SYR of someone you might not be interested in. Many years later you will run into these people and be happy for the connection. Stay up all night talking and laughing with your roommates, your time living together is short.

Explore your faith. Just because you didn't grow up a practicing Catholic, use this time to ask questions. Understand the traditions, learn about Mass, then you will know enough to make an educated decision for yourself. Don't be self-conscious, you will come to learn that faith is about values, and you share the same values as many of those around you.

Your life may be hard. You'll question why this is. You will keep a tight eye on the money you earn from your on-campus job, that's all you have. Classes will seem so much harder than in high school. You won't have the family contacts to help you secure internships. But don't discount your greatest qualities that you gained from working hard for what you have. Your friends may seem more mature, more experienced, more worldly, but you should know that they love and admire you for your unique qualities in the same way you look up to them. You may not be able to see this clearly, but you are unique and equal. Thousands of others tried to be one of the lucky freshmen at Notre Dame, but there was something extraordinary about you that the University spotted. So, give of yourself. Contribute to the community. Soak in every day, every memory. Be grateful for all you have been given, every single day.

You deserve to be here, and don't forget that. You may come from a blue-collar, low-income home, most of your friends attend community college, if any college at all, but you worked for this, you can do it, and you deserve it. Everyone has insecurities, even if you don't see them. Don't let that hold you back. Dad always said that with a good education you can make anything for yourself. And you do. Because of Notre Dame, you will be able to become the person you always wanted to be.

Participate in the Notre Dame Family, it's one that will fulfill you for your entire life. Be proud yet humble of this extraordinary community to which you belong. You will meet many people connected to the University in the years to come, and they will always make you feel welcome.

Your life does not turn out exactly as you had planned, it's not perfect. You made some career decisions and then changed your mind. You regret how you acted in some situations. You do not have the perfect double income family with 2.5 kids and a white picket fence. But the risks you took and the lessons you learned were worth it. You are happy. You are very, very happy. And you have more love in your life than you could have ever imagined. Starting today, every single day state three things you are grateful for, and it will be the key to your happiness.

Life Is Good,

Your future self

Christina Glorioso '95, '99
Bachelor of Business Administration,
Finance and MBA in Marketing

Christina is a single mom of four sons under the age of 6! Christina serves on the Monogram Club Board of Directors, on the Deans Advisory Council of the Mendoza College of Business, and was honored as a "Distinguished Alumni" by Mendoza. After being a Finance undergrad major and working in technology, she went back to ND for her MBA and started her career in Entertainment Marketing. She is currently Senior Vice President of Integrated Marketing at NBCUniversal, overseeing sales marketing for TODAY, Nightly News, Meet the Press, MSNBC and CNBC as well as a local small business owner. Prior to starting her family, Christina earned her Master Diver SCUBB certification and has summited Mount Kilimanjaro. But what she has loved (and still loves) to do most is mentor hundreds of Notre Dame students and recent graduates over the years.

Give your life back to the world

Dear Freshman Self,

Freshman year was marked by so much excitement and trepidation about college and the future. I would offer these pieces of advice to guide you in navigating all that I would encounter:

Follow your Heart's Desire. Listen to what really interests you and pursue it in every way you can, even if it does not make sense to others. History has shown that people who had the courage to listen to that inner call have done amazing things that would not have happened if they ignored it and did what the external world told them they should do. God's call is speaking to you through what your heart desires.

Seek to be good, not great. As one of my spiritual directors wisely said to me along the way: "What God asks of you is to be as good as you can at whatever you do. Greatness might be conferred on you, but that is not under your control or even the most important thing. Seeking to be great will actually interfere with your quest."

Form and rely on your own Council of Elders. Some call this your personal "Board of Directors," but that is more of a corporate term. I prefer Council of Elders because what is at stake is the care of your life as a precious gift, not a business commodity to be shaped by strategic planning and the overemphasis on "being successful." Your life has been given to you so that you can make the best of it and give it back to the world. Find a variety of people (young and old) who represent different parts of your life and who are totally dedicated to your being the person you really are. When you go through hard times or big decisions, seek out some of those people as you work through whatever you're going through. Those trusted people can help you discern how to navigate your life's journey and support you through it.

If you center your life on compassion, you will be happy. We humans were built for compassion. We are built to be interdependent. The most fulfilling part of life will be when you respond to the suffering of others. But it is also important that you are compassionate to yourself and that you let yourself receive compassion from others when they try to help you.

When times become darker, let your light shine more brightly. You will encounter tough times and some people who do not wish you well. It will be easy to become demoralized and want to quit. As Winston Churchill said, "If you're going through hell, keep going...." So be wise about whom you allow access to your inner spirit. When something doesn't feel right, listen to that, take action to protect yourself, find ways to keep your spirit up in the dark times.

You have nothing to lose. Go for it. Spending time dwelling on your faults and fears is a waste of time. Yes, do learn from them, but don't let them stop you from doing what you are called to do. Your mistakes and setbacks can teach you the most important information to make you succeed in your journey. Reaching for your goals may actually lead to better things of which you were not even aware. God's working in your life is real. You will be amazed how God guided you and accompanied you through your life journey even when you thought you had failed. It will all make sense eventually. Embrace the story that is your life.

Dominic

Dominic O. Vachon '80 '85
Bachelor of Arts in Psychology and Philosophy,
and Masters in Divinity

Dominic O. Vachon M.Div., Ph.D. is the Director of the Ruth M. Hillebrand Center for Compassionate Care in Medicine at Notre Dame and a practicing medical psychologist. He has spent most of his career training people in the health professions, teaching, and doing therapy. He graduated from Notre Dame in 1980 and 1985 and earned his doctorate at Loyola University of Chicago in 1993.

Embrace who you are — not despite the labels, but in light of them

Dear Freshman Self,

Your senior year of high school you felt unapologetically ambitious, like no obstacle could deter your predetermined course of success. You were top of your class, a youth group leader, admitted to one of the country's best colleges, and you had just learned to drive a stick shift. Walking onto Notre Dame's campus you will feel confident in your ability to succeed and change the world. But in just the first week, your enthusiasm will begin to fade. You'll face the harsh reality that is a "minority" status. I know you understand a minority status intellectually. You can define it, give examples, analyze the term and the groups characterized by it, sure, but you have yet to live it. Growing up in Los Angeles, "Latina" and "low socioeconomic status" were labels with no tangible significance. You understand your identity consists of your personhood, not these external qualifiers. They are relevant in applications or census data, not your interpersonal relationships. I want to warn you that a different understanding of the term will manifest when you embody it daily.

For example, your classmate in Chemistry lab will prefer to ask a fellow white male student across the room for help before asking you who is standing right next to him. At first you'll think to yourself: Maybe they know each other or maybe I just look particularly intimidating today. But after several instances of being overlooked, you will begin to wonder why they assume you don't know the answer. Then at Milkshake Mass, the Sign of Peace won't be offered to you or your friends. Specifically, the boys in front of you will shake everyone else's hand but won't turn around to shake yours. Take the initiative to tap them on the shoulder and extend your hand to them. Do not stand to be overlooked in Mass, a space meant to be a place of equality.

But Kathy, don't let this discourage you. Make it your mission to regain the confidence you had in Los Angeles, not despite the labels but in light of them. I want you to embrace the reality of your minority status as evidence that our places in society are not fixed. Do this because your time at Notre Dame will be beautiful even if these small incidences boil your blood.

Father Ted Hesburgh will inspire you and comfort you. You don't know who Father Ted is yet, but let me tell you this man was a saint. Not only was he an advocate for social justice, he also cared deeply about the students at Notre Dame, regardless of color or background. In fact, it's because of him that women were admitted to the University. He embodies what Notre Dame stands for and that will inspire you like nothing else.

The friends you make this year will become your second family. You are going through this struggle together, facing similar challenges and similar prejudices. But the faith you have in each other and in God will carry you through any and all adversities.

Believe me, this year you will be angry, frustrated, and overwhelmed, but you will also feel loved and hopeful. The challenges you will face will make you stronger and you will feel excited to learn more about yourself and the world around you in the years to come.

Kathy

Kathy Casillas '20

Bachelor of Science in Neuroscience and Behavior

Kathy Casillas grew up in Los Angeles, California. She is currently a sophomore in the College of Science studying Neuroscience and Behavior with a minor in Sociology. After graduating from Notre Dame, Kathy aspires to earn a PhD and conduct interdisciplinary research of human behavior integrating social, cognitive, and neurological levels of analysis.

Don't quit, give yourself time to adjust

Dear Bob,

If you met me these days, you'd probably think I bleed blue and gold. And that'd be a fair assumption. I recently served on Notre Dame's Board of Trustees and I now serve on the Keough School's advisory council. I enjoy coming back for football games and I'm part of a long family legacy at the University. My mother, a Notre Dame Law School graduate, is even named Dillon, since one of her great-great uncles was Rev. Patrick Dillon, C.S.C., president of Notre Dame during the Civil War.

It's a perfect Notre Dame story.

But during my first semester, I almost left.

It was tough. After being a star student at a big public high school near Philadelphia, I found myself lost among countless stars in Indiana. It was hard to make friends. My cramped room at Zahm seemed to be designed for one person, yet I had two roommates, both with wildly different schedules. My twin brother James hadn't been accepted to Notre Dame, leaving me miffed about the place from the start. Looking for something to do, I sought out a reporting job at *The Observer*, but it didn't click.

As the humdrum 2004 football season dragged on— the Irish went 6-6 in Ty Willingham's final season—I began to think about transferring. Notre Dame was phony, I told myself, and I might as well head back to Pennsylvania and be with people I liked, maybe at Temple University or Penn State. I felt surrounded by well-dressed, good-looking and athletic students from around the country who were fitting in just fine and loving every minute. Meanwhile, I sat in the computer lab in the student center most nights in a hoodie, clicking through political news and listening to the Dave Matthews Band.

On the phone with my parents one night, they said they'd support me if I left Notre Dame, but urged me not to leave too abruptly. They told me to think it through and try to enjoy college a little more, to be less grouchy and less tense. I reluctantly agreed and shelved the transfer applications. Throughout the rest of my freshman year, I slogged on, slowly appreciating my classes and the people I met.

An epiphany or some magic moment where I suddenly fell in love with Notre Dame on a walk by the lakes as I listened to the *Rudy* soundtrack never came. There was simply that quiet decision on a winter evening not to quit. But that was everything. By choosing to stay, I challenged myself to adapt and change, to plow through small grievances and many mistakes and to keep on, to be a man.

It paid off: my brother James eventually transferred in and we both majored in American Studies. During senior year, we lived in Dillon Hall and he was my resident assistant. My sister Ellen was a freshman at Notre Dame by then and lived across South quad. I ended up interviewing Dave Matthews for *The Observer*. Rev. John Jenkins, C.S.C., became a friend and mentor along the way.

My advice to you: don't quit. Freshman year isn't easy, and Notre Dame isn't perfect. But give it time. Give yourself time.

Robert Costa '08
Bachelor of Arts in American Studies

Robert Costa is a national political reporter for the Washington Post, *moderator of PBS's "Washington Week," and a political analyst for NBC News and MSNBC. He covers the White House and Congress, and frequently appears on "Meet the Press" and "Morning Joe."* Washingtonian *magazine has said he is "one of the next generation of journalists worth following." He is a 2008 graduate of the University of Notre Dame and earned a master's degree in politics in 2009 from the University of Cambridge, where he studied Winston Churchill.*

Commit yourself to learning
for the sake of learning

Dear Freshman Claire,

Four years. That's the amount of precious time you get to call yourself a Notre Dame student. Count yourself lucky, drink up every second that you have, and take full advantage of every opportunity that comes your way.

It's easy for me to selectively forget how hard the transition is to a new academic and social environment (I've now done it twice in the past four years because you're fortunate enough to study abroad!), so I've included a few words of advice that I've learned, often through trial and error, about life generally and Notre Dame specifically:

Practice more introspection, about the big things especially. I found that it was easy to go through the motions, to follow an even course by playing it safe. Why are you studying engineering? How will your Notre Dame education (which also extends beyond the classroom) contribute to your goals in life? Are you happy with how you spend your time and the people you share your time with? To be frank, I still don't have fully developed answers to these heavy questions but thinking about them can nevertheless be fruitful. And if you find that you are unsatisfied with the answers you ascertain, take a risk and change something.

Actively engage in the various communities to which you belong—Notre Dame, your dorm, and South Bend. Apathy is a gateway to laziness and ignorance. Plus, you will meet such a diverse (in all senses of the word) group of friends.

Find passions separate from your circumstances and make time for them no matter where you are. Discover something you love to do irrespective of your studies and your friends, something that will feasibly entertain you through retirement! For example, I found that I love to go on long walks when the weather is beautiful - something that I took advantage of around the lakes here at Notre Dame, through the historic streets and scenic parks around Oxford, and along the Charles River in Boston.

The view that your time here at Notre Dame is only a vehicle to grad school or a lucrative job is frankly superficial (although, inevitably and thankfully, you will have a job at a wonderful company). I can't emphasize enough how important it is to commit yourself to learning for the sake of learning. I know it's hard, given the system of evaluation and examination, but staying curious and thirsty for knowledge, I've discovered at this point in my life, both makes me happy and a more effective learner. Part of the reason that it is so easy to fall into a routine of tailoring your studying toward a specific exam is your fear of failure. Failure is ok!! You will fail (Calculus III final exam, I'm looking at you), you will solve problems incorrectly, you will be frustrated and annoyed by the fact that you can't, for the life of you, comprehend the implications of Schrodinger's equation, but do NOT take the easy way out and give up.

You will grow from your failures and mistakes; your friends will still love you, you will still be able to study abroad, and you will manage to get a great job after graduation.

Through all the time you toil in the section lounge or at your desk, make sure to take enough time and effort for self-care. I know it's easier said than done, but too much fro-yo and not enough sleep does not make a happy Claire. Your mental and physical well-being is more important than any assignment or exam.

Do not get trapped under the Notre Dame bubble; we are vulnerable to sliding into this mindset, but there are simple patterns of behavior that inspire a general awareness of the world around you. Read the news and discuss current events and philosophical dilemmas with your friends... it's really not hard to do and you don't need to physically leave the bubble in order to do it.

To part, on a somewhat ironic note, don't let anyone else shape your expectations or definition of the "Notre Dame experience." Your experience is uniquely yours—you will have times of jubilation and celebration and sadness and disappointment; late nights studying and late nights socializing. You will meet friends that I hope to know for the rest of my life, fantastically talented, wickedly smart, and incredibly hilarious friends.

As I write this letter, only a few months from graduation, I look back on my time here at Notre Dame dearly; although I feel excited and prepared for the "real world," there is an undeniable part of me that would be lying if I didn't say that I will be very sad to dress in my cap and gown and receive that gilded Notre Dame diploma. Your admission letter warmly stated, "Welcome Home," and as a senior about to fly the nest, I can truly say that this place and these people are truly my home.

Love,

Senior Claire

Claire Gaffney '18
Bachelor of Science in Electrical Engineering

Claire is a senior Electrical Engineering major from Alexandria, Virginia. She lived in McGlinn Hall where she made best friends and study partners alike. After graduation, she plans to move to Chicago to work at Deloitte.

Just show up

Corey,

Welcome to South Bend. It's a lot different than south Texas, and that's okay. This adventure promises much, and I hope you eagerly embrace the good and bad. Looking back on my time at Notre Dame, three things continually emerge as blessings discovered too late. First, explore South Bend. Second, befriend your professors. Third, just show up.

My freshman year, I remember leaving South Bend to go to Chicago as often as I could. Not one of my classmates ever spoke about what South Bend had to offer. In fact, the city remained a mystery to me until I got involved with student government sophomore year. The more local coffee shops I frequented, the more charming the city became. The more events I attended in town, the more relationships I built. The more community members I spoke to, the more opportunities I saw for positive change through partnership. Bowling nights at Strikes and Spares bring back as many warm feelings as late night pizza at Reckers. Now when I think of home, I think of two places: San Antonio and South Bend. Invest where you are, and it will give back to you in multiples.

Professors always seemed so scary, like judges sternly delivering definitive assessments on my abilities. The thought of spending time with them outside class terrified me. Talk about being wrong! Some of my favorite memories are watching soccer games with athletic administrators, coffee with my psychology professor at LaFun, dinner in Jerusalem with study abroad faculty, or lunch in town with my friend's rector. Build relationships with faculty and staff. They're some of the most fascinating and kind individuals I've met, and I'm thankful to call them my friends.

Lastly, just show up. You'd be surprised how many people don't show up—all for legitimate reasons too. If you show up, you're putting yourself in a position for success because you're giving yourself the opportunity to be successful. Don't be afraid what people might think, or if you feel you might make a fool of yourself. A lot of the time your presence speaks volumes to your interest and commitment in a subject matter, even if you can't speak eloquently on it. The best thing I ever did in school was show up to random events I never thought I'd attend. It's a great way to meet new people, develop new interests, and challenge your comfort zone.

Have fun and keep these tips in mind. Don't stress! Most things will work themselves out in time. You'll have a blast. The next few years won't be easy, but they'll be some of the most rewarding, exciting years of your life.

Corey

Corey Robinson '17
Bachelor of Arts in the Program of
Liberal Studies and Sustainability

Corey graduated from the University of Notre Dame in 2017, finishing with a varsity letter in football and a degree in the Program of Liberal Studies and Sustainability. After a string of concussions ended a three-year playing career at wide receiver, he stepped away from the game becoming both a student assistant coach and Student Body President in his final year. Corey co-founded a national non-profit, One Shirt One Body, with friend and creative visionary Andrew Helmin. One Shirt One Body promotes the pursuit of higher education through the donation of issued gear by college athletes into their local communities. Other honors include Rhodes Scholar finalist (2016), Capital One First Team Academic All-America (2014), and Indiana Bicentennial Torch Relay Bearer Honoree (2016). Corey is now living in New York full time, working in business development at Sotheby's, the world's leading auction house. In his free time, Corey enjoys writing screenplays and playing music with his band Rolfs Aquatic.

Be an activist for what you believe in

Freshman Tiffany,

I am coming to you, a near-sophomore, telling you that you're going to be fine. You're a fighter. Yes, Balfour and Welcome Weekend were two completely different experiences. Yes, you will find that you much prefer one over the other; I know you will think that someone pointing out your "nice Mexican hair" is the end of the world and reason enough to transfer. I know you will think that General Chemistry will be the death of you. I know you will even think that leaving Physics is the best idea, but you will find that your heart belongs there, even when you do eventually switch into Computer Science.

You will find the election season is hard. You wanted something so badly that you never got to see, and the effects are exactly what you predicted, if not worse. Some of your friends will be harassed for being Muslim, Hispanic, or undocumented. You're fine, though. You will find that this will bring out something that had been simmering within you for ages. You will realize that you are an activist, and that you believe strongly that every human being is valuable in their own right.

You will be homesick—homesick enough to call your parents and ask for a semester off. You won't take that semester off, but you almost do.

But, soon enough, you will become adjusted.

You will find friends outside of the small circles you're afraid to leave. You will go on retreats that will make you cry because you love everyone you met so much, and they are suddenly showing gratitude for you. You will meet friends with whom you will spend late nights talking, laughing, and wandering campus. You will make so many mistakes but bounce right back up, because that's what you do best. You will find a research position in physics. You will switch your major with all the heartbreak of knowing that both majors are right for you. You will take Chinese and love every minute of it despite the fact that you mess up more times than you can count in a five-minute span. You will find clubs with all of the people who made your Notre Dame experience turn into this wonderful thing.

In your freshman year, you will experience all the emotions that you need to in order to ensure you grow, not only as a person, but as one of the Fighting Irish. You will find your home under the Dome—that I promise you.

Sincerely,

Your Future Self

Tiffany Rojas
'20 Bachelor Arts
Computer Science and Engineering

Tiffany is an economics major from Duncanville, Texas, in the class of 2020. She is involved in 1stG ND, Diversity and Inclusion on Student Government, the Fighting Irish Scholars, and a Multicultural Commissioner in Breen-Phillips Hall. She has participated in physics undergraduate research. She takes great interest in studying Chinese, hoping to pursue it as a minor or second major.

Pursue decisions with your heart

Dear Freshman Self,

You're 17, six time zones from home, living in a so-called "triple" in the Freshmen Annex at St. Ed's, watching upper-classmen supervising cockroach races in the hallway, and wondering what the next four years have in store. Take my word for it, you'll soon fall in love with this place, even on hot days with no air conditioning. As great as your freshman year is, sophomore year gets even better as ND will admit women! You'll be intimidated by the lopsided male-female ratio, and be hesitant to ask these women for dates, fearing rejection, but "just do it." To your surprise, they'll say "Yes"!

Pursue a major with your heart, not your mind, and later do the same when choosing a career. If you enjoy your work and homework (most of the time, anyway), you'll en-joy your life's journey more, plus you'll be more successful as a result.

If a professor is outstanding, take him or her for more courses, as you'll remember the lessons best that you learned from a teacher who engages and inspires you. Given your many years studying *The Baltimore Catechism*, you're not thrilled with the two-theology course requirement but take the opportunity to study another faith at Notre Dame, like Islam. It will help you in business and in your personal life and contribute to your understanding of the world.

30

A Notre Dame education is a blessing and usually leads to a good white-collar job after graduation. Use your summers to get your hands dirty working alongside blue-collar workers. You'll acquire a special appreciation for the difficulty of their work and what these strong people do for our country and economy.

Set high life goals. Work hard. Don't settle for mediocrity. Strive to make a difference in the world.

Have fun and develop real friendships. The memories of the fun you had together will strengthen the bond you feel with true friends made, and these reflections will provide a valuable nutrient for your mind and psyche throughout your life.

And finally, you'll snicker about Notre Dame alumni and how silly and fashion-challenged they are as they walk around campus on football weekends in their garish green, blue and gold, and you'll swear you'll never look like that. I've got some really bad news for you...

Sincerely,

Your much older and slightly wiser self

Dan Hesse '75
Bachelor of Arts in Government and Liberal Studies
Dan Hesse currently serves as a member of the board of directors of PNC Financial Services Group, Inc. (NYSE: PNC) and Akamai Technologies (NASDAQ: AKAM). Dan served as President and CEO of Sprint Corporation from December 2007 to August 2014. Previously, Hesse was the Chairman and CEO of Embarq Corporation, a $6 billion telecommunications services company. From 2000-2004, he served as Chairman, President and CEO of Terabeam Corporation, a wireless telecommunications technology company. Hesse spent 23 years at AT&T. From 1997-2000, he served as the President

and CEO of AT&T Wireless Services, at the time the United States'
largest wireless carrier. He served as a member of the board of directors
of VF Corporation from 1999-2008 and of Nokia from 2005-2007.
He received a BA from Notre Dame, an MBA from Cornell, and an
MS from MIT where he was awarded the Brooks Thesis Prize. He
holds a Carnegie Mellon University/NACD CERT certificate in Cy-
bersecurity Oversight. He serves on the National Board of Governors of
the Boys & Girls Clubs of America, the board of directors of the JUST
Capital Foundation, and on the advisory boards of the New York
Global Leaders Dialogue and of Rutberg and Company. In addition
to receiving Corporate Responsibility Magazine's Lifetime Achievement Award, he has been named "Most Influential Person in Mobile
Technology" by LAPTOP magazine (Steve Jobs was #2).

Live during the weeks,
and not just for the weekends

Dear Freshman Self,

Don't be surprised when, before you know it, you are almost no longer a freshman. If I could offer you one piece of advice, it would be to live during the weeks, and not just for the weekends (although it's not like you will be doing anything particularly wild on the weekends—what I mean is not to have the mindset that you only have to get through the work of the week, in order to experience a brief respite from endless work). In fact, I would tell you to work on the weekend so that you can enjoy your weeks. After all, weekdays constitute five-sevenths of our lives! Now, while I would love to tell you that this means that you should get all of your homework for the week done on the weekends, that just will not be possible. So, by "living" during the week, I mean that you should not see what you have to do simply as something that you *have* to do, but as your life. You are doing it because that is what you are *doing*, that is how you are *living*, so enjoy it! You'll soon realize that there is never a time when there is nothing to do, and that the way you can make the most of your Notre Dame education is not to live thinking that you can finish everything so that you can enjoy yourself, but to live thinking that you can enjoy yourself in what you are doing in that moment. Strengthening your *mind* is, after all, a primary purpose of education.

33

Continue to believe that what you do in your classes is directly connected to what you do outside of them. As a theology major, keep seeing that what you learn in class about God can help you when you are in Mass, or at Vespers, to listen to God. The seemingly mundane lecture notes that you type up every week have a direct connection to the seemingly mundane movements of your heart each week.

Don't be afraid that you've lost your *zeal* for your faith. Just because it is easy to share faith here, and you may not have many opportunities to share your faith with someone who does not know or understand, does not mean that you are less faithful. Now is the time to fortify, later will be the time to be tested. It is okay to enjoy something now, like the first-ever Right to Life SYR, with crazy, fun people who love and respect life, knowing that when you go out into the world later people will not be as receptive to your beliefs.

Accept and appreciate that it is okay to extend the way you love to the friends you meet—to a new, extended family. You are not loving your family less by loving others also. And, most important, that love can merge when your family gets to meet your friends and you get to meet your friends' families. Opportunities like Lewis Hall's Dad's Weekend will give you a chance to do this.

And keep always in perspective God's providential love, which exists in and through whatever tough times you may encounter. Just like the bracelet you will wear on your left hand says, "Pray Like a Champion Today," your ultimate purpose is to pray like a champion, to be a saint, and to *hope* no matter what life throws at you. And at Our Lady's University, Our Lady will always help you do this.

Love forever,

Your one-year wiser (sillier?) self

Noelle Johnson '20
Bachelor of Arts in Theology and Physics

Noelle Johnson is a Theology and Physics double major from Los Ange- les in the Glynn Family Honors Program, and a Suzanne and Walter Scott Scholar. Outside of class, she is a Sorin Fellow with the Center for Ethics and Culture, which gave her the opportunity and funding to intern at the Archdiocese of Los Angeles' Office of Life, Justice, and Peace in the summer of 2017, as well as ND Right to Life's Apologetics commissioner. Currently she is pursuing her passion, the complemen- tarity of faith and reason, as an intern for the McGrath Institute for Church Life's Science and Religion Initiative. She hopes eventually to be a Theology professor and it is her dream to work at or for the Vatican in some way.

Be comfortable being uncomfortable

Reina,

You once asked your good friend Rachel how she could possibly enjoy running cross country. You can picture her laughing and shaking her head. Rachel told you that you just had to be comfortable being uncomfortable. Little did you know that this simple and seemingly contradictory piece of advice would evolve to mean so much to you.

I wish I could say that you are overcome with joy at the prospect of beginning your education at Notre Dame, as anyone lucky enough to be in your shoes should be. However, there is a lot of sadness weighing you down. You're far from home, from your friends, and the perfect San Diego weather, in this weird landlocked state full of corn and devoid of good Mexican food (Abuelita save me!). You have parted ways from your very best friends and being 1,111 miles away from them took a little fun out of being welcomed home to the most gorgeous of all college campuses. Know that you will overcome the fear and grief that seem so monumental right now.

You have learned how to listen to your body. Believe it or not, you cannot run on four hours of sleep every night. (Trust me, you'll end up asleep in Gen Chem and cursing whoever scheduled you for an 8:20 theology class.) You will learn that you need exercise. Soccer and CrossFit have always been great loves of yours, and you'll come to realize that you can't live without them. You will learn that you are not alone. Your hallmates, as well as a very special St. Mary's girl, stand by you in all things, but Christ himself walks beside you. The spiritual transformation you will undergo in your first year here will change your entire life for the better. There will be moments when God picks you up and carries you, and others when Jesus will hold your hand as you struggle.

You could never guess from where you are standing how Notre Dame will envelop you. Being one of the Fighting Irish will be forever ingrained in your person, and in your heart. You will feel an unspeakable joy in singing the Alma Mater, knowing that you are part of something so full of goodness and love. You will spend countless hours studying at Reckers, consuming ridiculous amounts of their cheese pizza and energy-boosted smoothies, often after two in the morning. You will battle through two sets of finals. You will push through crowds to hug every person you know in the Dillon chapel during the Sign of Peace at Milkshake Mass each week. You will come to see this place as your home under the Dome.

College will be harder than you have ever imagined it could be. You will run on less sleep and more caffeine than you thought possible or healthy (it's not healthy, please sleep, get all the sleep you can). You will cry so much. Your heart will be broken and stitched back up again. You will say *a lot* of Hail Mary's. You will be confirmed in faith. You will fall in love with college, Notre Dame, Christ, and you will come to love yourself in a way that you never thought possible. You will spend the vast majority of your time overwhelmed, drowning, and supremely uncomfortable. Pushed to your limits, you will grow. Somehow, you will get comfortable being uncomfortable, and it will be part of what makes you great.

Sincerely,

Reina

Reina Koran '20
Bachelor of Science in Biochemistry
Reina is a sophomore biochemistry major from San Diego. She aspires to attend graduate school and pursue medical research in the field of regenerative medicine. She is involved in undergraduate research on campus, is involved in her hall government, and is part of Matriculate advising fellows mentoring high school students. Her outside interests include soccer, art and music.

Open your aperture

Dear Matt,

I am writing this letter almost 20 years after you have graduated from Notre Dame. I will try to be brief... there are so many topics to cover, but overall the five below seem like good words of guidance as you enter your freshman year:

1. **Open your aperture.** Meet as many people as you can and work hard to extend your social community. Do not limit yourself by associating with students who only think and act like you. You will learn later in life that different perspectives, different communication styles, and different personalities are what drive great ideas. There are so many unique and talented people at Notre Dame . . . meet and learn from as many as you can. Don't just "accept" the vast individuality that is inherent in the ND student body . . . seek out and embrace that individuality.

2. **Enjoy your friends** . . . spend as much time as you can with them. You will be moving your family of five 18 years later and, as part of the usual task of throwing so many things out, you will come across a picture of two close friends, hanging out on your porch on Navarre Street. Both will have unexpectedly passed away well before they were 40. You will say to yourself: "Man, I wish I could go back to that day . . ." Own the times you have with your close friends . . . listen to them and make sure they know how important they are to you.

3. Embrace the many challenging moments you will experience as a new member of the Men's Soccer team . . . you may not realize it then, but those hard lessons are what prepare you most for the professional world. Literally everything you achieve in your professional career for the next 20 years is due to the team around you. Learn how to collaborate and motivate as much as you can . . . take time to elevate your teammates and work to improve the team every day.

4. Go home early! A wise man once told my girlfriend (now wife) at ND, ". . . nothing good happens after 2:00 AM . . ."; boy was he right. When out on a weekend, try to regularly cut the night short and go home as much as you can—you won't regret it.

5. Savor the lazy Sundays and commit to watching *Goodfellas, Braveheart* and *The Godfather* at least once per quarter while eating Papa John's in your dorm room. Soon, with three little children, your movie options take a turn for the worse . . . *Madagascar, Jumanji,* or *Night at the Museum.* While still fun, it just isn't the same.

Enjoy the next four years . . . there are so many amazing students to meet and teachers to learn from. Make the most of it and embrace every day!

Matt

Matt Zimmer '98
Bachelor of Business Administration, Accounting
Matt Zimmer graduated from the University of Notre Dame in 1998 and majored in Accounting. Matt began his career at PwC and subsequently entered investment banking by joining Robert W. Baird. Matt later joined William Blair & Company, a global boutique investment bank, and has spent time in Blair's U.S. and European offices. Today,

Matt is a partner at William Blair and is the Global Head of Services and Industrials. Matt and his wife Marny (ND '98) live in Chicago with their three young children, Patrick, Rhett, and Will.

Find what interests you and do it

Dear Emily,

"Go confidently in the direction of your dreams. Live the life you have imagined." The best advice you've ever received was this Henry David Thoreau quote that your mom put in your senior yearbook. Embrace these words and get ready to begin your next four years at Notre Dame. Here are a few pieces of advice I want to give you to help you along this journey.

Remember the things that you believe in now and get ready for many of those things to change. Your understanding of yourself and the world around you is about to be pushed, pulled, twisted, and molded into something entirely new. This transformation does not happen overnight, nor does it happen with big, life-changing events. It happens slowly, with each late-night study session, each casual dining hall conversation, and every interaction with every person you happen to meet. At the end of it all, you will be able to look back on your experience and see that the things that meant the most were the ones that at first meant nothing at all.

Find the places where you can be your best self. These places, whether a physical location or an event or a club that you get involved in, will be what defines you and your college experience. You will find comfort and strength in a beautiful group of girls who share a passion for performance, developed over many nights in Washington Hall. You will find intellectual stimulation and inspiration through a small entrance to Brownson Hall. And you will find your favorite place to do your work, eat your lunch, and study for exams. This location in Stepan Hall, often used by students as a throughway to avoid the bitter South Bend winters, will be the place where you laugh and cry, and where friendships will inevitably bloom. These places will be the places where people go to find you and, when you come back to visit as an alum, they will be the places you want to go.

Follow your instincts and do things you think you should do, even when they don't seem to fit in your "plans." Everything that you do will influence you. Apply for the program that you think is interesting. Take the class on Australian History. Do research for a priest on the philosophy of biology. Not everything that you do needs to be solely based on what you think your career is. Take advantage of these opportunities and carry them with you in the future.

Lastly, enjoy your four years while they last! Writing this as a recently graduated Emily, I am missing my home under the Dome terribly. Frequently look at the Golden Dome and remember how blessed you are to be where you are. Love big and love often. And finally, cherish the friends and memories that you make. They will mean more to you than you know.

And as always, go Irish!

Love,

A slightly older, maybe wiser Emily

Emily Zion '17
Bachelor of Science in Biology

Emily Zion is a 2017 alumna, who is originally from Northville, Michigan and is now residing in Baltimore, Maryland. She is currently pursuing a PhD in Biology at the Johns Hopkins University, where she is beginning a five-year journey in scientific research. After obtaining her PhD, Emily hopes to pursue a career in academia where she can continue research as well as teach biology courses at the university level. In her free time, she enjoys dancing, traveling, and participating in science outreach programs such as SABES.

Focus on breaking your own limits

Dear Bridget,

Pause for a second, gaze up at the Dome, take a deep breath and smile. You've accomplished your lifelong dream of attending Notre Dame. Be proud of that! You are extremely well-prepared, but here are some suggestions as you embark on four of the best years of your life:

Recognize the significance of this opportunity and the moments that make it special. College isn't preparation for a job; it's preparation for life, so decide what your goals are and make the most of this time. This is the perfect chance to explore and pursue the activities that interest you most. You'll strengthen skill sets that will lead to a career and make friends you wouldn't have met otherwise. Graduation will be here before you know it, so build a foundation that will serve you well down the road. In the meantime, enjoy the little things like waking up to the band marching across campus on game day, road trips, dorm Masses, walks around campus and Professor McKenna's tap class.

Cultivate and cherish relationships. You'll rehash the night's events over Papa John's breadsticks in Farley's hallway at 3 a.m. with your friends. You'll drop into their room for impromptu dance parties. Sure, maybe you should be sleeping or finishing a paper, but you're also building friendships with the women who will stand beside you at your wedding and encourage you through life's highs and lows. Years from now, when you all live in different cities, you'll realize that this time was a gift. Get to know your professors and learn from the wisdom that surrounds you. You are now part of the Notre Dame family, so cultivate that built-in community. Joining your alumni club after graduation will open doors and enrich your life in countless ways.

Be grateful. Count your blessings. On mornings when you'd rather pull the covers over your head than face whatever challenges await, step back and remember that you're getting a fantastic education at your dream school. You have access to opportunities that many people could only hope for, a supportive family, friends who love you for you, and thousands of alumni to lean on professionally and personally. Know that you'll tackle whatever obstacles you encounter. When you need to be reminded of the strength that lies within or how fortunate you are, spend an hour at the Grotto (or call your parents). Or both.

Trust your heart and focus less on everyone else. Choose the major that interests you and don't worry that you don't have a set "path" like your classmates majoring in medicine or accounting. Your path will be whatever you make it, even if it isn't a straight line. What matters more than a major is whether you have a strong work ethic, emotional intelligence, and the ability to contribute to a team, communicate clearly and think critically. Don't waste time comparing yourself to others. There will always be someone smarter, more accomplished, better looking, etc. Instead, focus on breaking your own limits. Judge yourself based on how much you've grown. You'll be happier in the long run.

Study abroad. Yes, you will miss campus and your friends. You'll sit alone at the Grotto, terrified about what you've gotten yourself into. Why would you want to move to a foreign country and live with a family you've never met? News flash—not only will you survive, but it will be one of the most transformational and unbelievable experiences of your life.

Remember, if you make good choices, stay rooted in your values and trust yourself, you can accomplish anything.

Go Irish!

Bridget

Bridget Veihmeyer '05
Bachelor of Arts in American Studies

Bridget Veihmeyer Monahan majored in American Studies and Spanish at Notre Dame. She is currently a senior marketing specialist in Bethesda, Maryland, where she directs D.C. metro area marketing and public relations efforts at United Bank. Throughout her career in communications, Bridget has held various positions at ESPN, HBO, Disney On Ice and Bank of Georgetown. Currently, she is president of the Notre Dame Club of Washington, D.C.

Be real, be authentic, keep your head up

Dear Freshman Bill,

Don't worry. You're not a fraud and no one is going to find out that you have been faking that you were smart all along. You are actually smarter than you believe, but I'll get to that later. Right now, you should study much more than you think you need to. It turns out that you're not that strong of a "studier." You will come to find out the C stands for Chemistry and it turns out it's not all that bad. In the words of Thornton Melon, who was trying to reassure his son, "A, B, C . . . you're in the top three, why are you so worried?" It turns out that many years later, you will get plenty of credit for graduating with a degree in Electrical Engineering. No one will ever ask you about your GPA!

Here is some other advice you probably won't take: Be real, authentic, and even a little vulnerable with your roommates, classmates, and ROTC friends. None of them will use that information against you. They are actually all here to help you get through. Feel free to tell your roommate how unjust the grading of your Physics exam was and how you are doubting you can make it through another class, let alone another mid-term and even the semester. You don't need to hide in the basement bathroom and cry because you don't know how to succeed. You don't need to keep pretending you don't need help. Share with your roommates that you called your mom crying because you didn't think you could do it anymore and she sternly asked "What? Do you want me to come pick you up?" You can do it. It won't be easy, and you will walk the campus with a sense of impending doom of failing the midterms. The community support will become evident to you when a junior asks you "Are you looking for change?" because your head is aimed straight toward the ground. He'll say, with a big smile, "Keep your head up!" And that will be enough to keep you going. You will do it and you won't actually fail any midterms.

While I'm giving you all this advice, here is some more that you should take to heart. Make sure you go to every dorm Mass you can in the next four years. You will spend the rest of your life trying to find the spiritual equivalent and you will come to realize it's only available those four years. I know, four years sounds like a long time, but you'll figure out how fast it goes right when it's over. The community you will build in your short time at Our Lady's University will support you the rest of your life. Those friendships will be forged during all those late-night hearts games after the dorm Mass. Those same friends will wonder out loud how you graduated with a degree in engineering when they never saw you sit down and study. You'll be grateful for the opportunities your degree provides later in life, even if you're not so grateful taking the GPA beating that you are about to face.

Listen to me now and believe me later. Two consecutive SYRs is no reason to start planning your future life together and naming your four future children. Ah yes, you will never quite understand Notre Dating. And that's ok. The love of your life, and the mother of those four children lives in Texas right now. You won't meet her here on campus, like you always imagined. John Hughes was never telling the truth in those movies. God has a better plan for you.

You will find out one day that you really don't know anything about life. And the more you figure out what you do know, the more and more you realize how little you know about anything significant. Notre Dame will make you want to be a better person than you ever thought possible. You will continue to struggle to know what you are called to do. But the fact that you are even concerned with fulfilling that call is something you will owe to Notre Dame for the rest of your life. It will awaken in you a desire to do the best and be the best, not just for personal glory but for the greater good.

You don't even know how awesome, terrifying, and life-changing these next four years will be. I know I have given you a lot of different advice, but don't change a thing. It's all prologue to where you are now. Where you are now is awesome—not perfect, but awesome!

Respectfully,

A much older Bill

Bill Kempf '94
Bachelor of Science in Electrical Engineering
Bill Kempf is a Regional Development officer for the University of Notre Dame who works with families in Texas and Oklahoma. Bill served seven years in the Air Force in California and Texas. Accolades, such as Captain of the Irish Guard and Mr. Stanford Hall, have prepared him well to be a current Moreau FYE instructor. Bill lives in South Bend with his wife Susan and is the proud father of four hopeful future Domers. He is also the proud uncle of two Notre Dame alumni, Hunter Kempf '17 and Max Kempf '17, and the world's best godfather to current student, Haley Kempf '20.

Treasure your experiences

Dear Nancy,

You lucky, lucky girl! I know you are incredibly excited to be a freshman (Class of '84) at Notre Dame ... as you should be. What a gift it is to be young and wide-eyed, following in the footsteps of your dad, brother and sister, embarking on a four-year adventure at the most beautiful, storied University in the world.

Although it is thrilling to have your first taste of independence . . . SLOW DOWN and take better care of yourself! Stop procrastinating and pulling all-nighters. Eat healthier, and exercise more—A LOT more. (I know, I know—that's not really "a thing" yet but trust me—it will be.) Pace yourself, kid. You don't have to go full-throttle, full-volume all the time. Find more quiet moments and quiet places to soak in what you have there, and to be grateful.

Believe me, I love that you have fully embraced what it means to be a Domer—no one yells louder at a football game or paints a shamrock on her face with more pride than you do. You'll be glad to know that feeling never goes away. In fact, it grows stronger—eventually you will become a fiercely proud Notre Dame parent, and you and your ND friends will get to teach your daughter (Class of '19) and her friends how to tailgate in style.

Speaking of those Notre Dame friends ... yours, Nancy, are the real "gold" under the Dome. Treasure them all. The friendships you make now will be the most important friendships of your lifetime. And the many magical (and often hilarious) memories you make together today will fuel you for decades to come. Seriously, you will still be laughing over the same stories with many of the same friends thirty years from now. (So make 'em count!)

A few other pieces of advice from someone who's been there. Don't forego the chance to study abroad. It is perhaps the most extraordinary opportunity Notre Dame will offer you, and even more essential today. Truth be told, not taking advantage of that opportunity is the only thing I regret about my own Notre Dame experience. (If I remember correctly, I was simply having too much fun at the time to consider a semester abroad. Ah, youth!)

This will not be your first instinct but try to spend more one-on-one time with your American Studies professors. So many of them are remarkable people with remarkable things to teach you, even beyond the classroom. Try to form closer connections and try to stay in touch after graduation.

Finally, as cliché as it sounds, don't take any of it for granted. Yes, the coursework can be grueling (even for an American Studies major). Yes, Walsh Hall can sometimes feel like ... a real fixer-upper. (One day they will renovate it, I'm sure.) Yes, you will have your heart broken on more than one occasion (all part of the journey). But, you won the lottery when you got that Notre Dame acceptance letter. And one day you will look back and realize that you would trade almost anything to do it all over again.

Until then, have fun, study hard (you can do both), and be well, my freshman self!

Love,

Me (older, wiser, and still lucky)

PS – One final piece of advice that I suspect you'll ignore: do NOT participate in An Tostal mud wrestling. (It's not worth the dislocated shoulder.)

Nancy Ruscheinski '84
Bachelor of Arts in American Studies
Nancy Ruscheinski worked in a variety of capacities spanning nearly 29 years for Edelman, the world's largest public relations firm. She launched and led Edelman's digital practice (now a $175M business with 1,000+ people), served as president of our Midwest region, grew Edelman Chicago to become the largest PR firm in the city, and helped lead and grow Edelman U.S. during her tenure as president and COO from 2008-2011. She now works at Edelman's sister agency, Zeno, as its first global Chief Operating Officer. She is known to enjoy relaxing with her family and dogs at their lakeside cottage in Michigan.

Live your life excited for every moment

Dear Freshman Kiley,

Make your alarm clock noise something you enjoy waking up to every morning. And when you wake up, ask yourself the question, "What am I excited to do today?" If you don't have an honest answer, make a change! College—and life—are too short to be spent doing things that don't make you feel fully alive. Always eat breakfast, especially before morning exams!

Know that a three-hour Sunday brunch with friends will not ruin your productivity for the day, it will only rejuvenate you for the week to come. If you have extra Flex Points come May, throw your friends a picnic on the quad. Make sure that you buy too much ice cream and offer it to passersbys who look like they could use some.

Always celebrate your friends' birthdays. Bake their favorite dessert in your dorm kitchen—don't buy it. If their birthday is over a school break, intentionally celebrate it when everyone is back. Know your friends' favorite snacks and leave them on their desk when they are out late studying. Know the names of their pets and siblings, too, and ask about them often.

When you go to dinner with your friends, leave your phone in your dorm. Sit in front of the Golden Dome on a perfectly sunny day without taking a single picture of it,

54

but do pick up that phone to call your mom when you're sad. Call her when you're happy. Call her for no particular reason and don't forget to call dad, too. Ask for directions your first week of class—it should never take an hour to find any building on campus. Figure out the South Bend bus system and get off campus for an entire day. Figure out another country and get off campus for an entire semester.

Know that it's OK to miss a football game and that it's OK to stay in on Friday (and Thursday and Saturday) nights—I did all those things and still have friends who blur into family.

Be unabashedly you, but also know that it's OK to constantly define and redefine yourself throughout this experience. Who you are now is not, and should not, be exactly who you are in four years. Do at least one activity that is completely foreign to you, and if you love it, stick with it. Be surprised! Don't trust that your eighteen-year-old self has the rest of your life figured out yet.

Ask questions and admit when you don't understand something. You didn't come to college because you already had all the answers. Ask people who are very different from you for book recommendations and ask them to coffee to discuss the book after you finish.

Practice gratitude—write thank you notes to professors who pour their heart into teaching you, and always, AL-WAYS, say thank you to dining hall and dorm staff. Keep a journal on your desk to jot down memories and advice you will want to share with others (but mostly yourself) in the years to come. I wrote, *for you*, last December in an entry unrelated to the weather, "Even South Bend's darkest winters have an end." Remember that.

Play music when you shower at night in the dorms—it makes the whole experience of having to wear sandals more tolerable. Drink a glass of water and take a deep breath before you go to sleep.

Try to love yourself like I have learned to love you,

Kiley

Kiley Adams '17
Bachelor of Science in Biology

Kiley graduated in 2017 with a major in Biological Sciences. She went to India twice during her undergraduate career to do research on the care, especially in rural communities, for people with disabilities. She is currently in India on the Fulbright Fellowship continuing this work. Outside of academics, Kiley played goalkeeper for the Notre Dame Women's Soccer program and is a 4th-degree Master black belt through the United States and World Taekwondo Federations.

Listen more, ask more, worry less

Dear Erin,

Listen more. Ask more. Worry less.

Listen more. You are surrounded by classmates who traveled from across the world, hold different views, bring varied cultural traditions, have unique talents, and display a range of economic backgrounds. You grew up in a small Wisconsin farming town of 1,200 where you knew most of your classmates from kindergarten through senior year. You visited only Chicago, Disney World, and Washington DC before coming to Notre Dame. Take more time to listen to the stories of those who will share the next four years with you. Living together in a community of randomly assigned residents is something unique to ND and offers an opportunity that you will never again be able to replicate. Do not take Siegfried women too much for granted while you are off concentrating on the next test or working in student government. Someday, the stories of people may be what you remember most.

Ask more. Rectors, professors, priests in residence, choir directors, club advisors, and administrators are not authority figures to pass in the hallway with a brief hello or consult only in times of need. No, you are not bothering Sr. Mo by stopping to talk. Professor Kaplan really meant that he hoped students would keep in touch. The seemingly straight path to majoring in accounting, a Big 8 summer internship, and an audit or tax job might not actually be right for you. Pause and ask yourself which classes you like best and why. Ask if there are other career options much earlier. Discuss your answers to these questions with those who have wisdom beyond your years. In other words, do not just follow a script because you think that it is the only way to get your student loans paid off. Years later, you will realize that professors, rectors, and even Student Affairs VPs have chosen to work at a University precisely to support your formation and assist in your discernment. They do not find talking to students an inconvenience. And Father Jenkins, one of the three professors you actually had the courage to talk with at office hours, might one day remember you and offer you an amazing job at your alma mater!

Worry less. Even with these tweaks, take heart. Some things you will actually get right the first time. It will take time to meet friends, but once you find them, they last. Melanie, Shaun, Sean, Brandon, Ed, Tracy and Stacy will be part of your life for decades. Laugh often. Stay up late. Savor the beauty of campus, especially at night or as the seasons change. Get free popcorn at the Oak Room, and do not be too sad when it closes to renovate South Dining Hall. Pray often at Siegfried and Zahm Hall Masses. Sing in Lit Choir (stop rolling your eyes, you grow to love it). Work hard. Take that lucky call from McKinsey. Try to be a servant leader. Know that the moment when ND will feel like home will come more quickly than you think in those first few scary and lonely months. Thank your Mom and Dad for the amazing opportunity and sacrifices they made so you could attend this special place. Have patience. Trust.

Open yourself to growing in both mind and heart. And dating your friend Ryan will turn out well.

With love,

Older you, who would do it all again in a heartbeat

Erin Hoffman Harding '97
Bachelor of Business Administration in Accounting

Erin Hoffmann Harding began her tenure as Vice President for Student Affairs in August 2012. As Vice President for Student Affairs Ms. Hoffmann Harding oversees five areas comprised of multiple departments related to residential life, student development, student services, campus ministry, and career and professional development. She previously served as associate vice president for strategic planning and special projects. Prior to coming to Notre Dame in 2005, Ms. Hoffmann Harding served as a management consultant in the Chicago and Cleveland offices of the international consulting firm McKinsey and Company Inc. She is a summa cum laude graduate of Notre Dame's Mendoza College of Business and earned her juris doctor degree magna cum laude from Harvard Law School. She and her husband, Ryan, also a Notre Dame graduate and an attorney, are the parents of three young sons.

Be vulnerable

Dear Freshman Emily,

Wow, you do not even know how exciting a year you have ahead of you. Although move-in started out a little rocky and you are not a fan of singing serenades and dancing in this hot weather, you are making memories that you will look back on all year (and probably beyond). I know that at this point you still think you are on top of the world. You are doing well in classes and have seemed to make some friends. Football games are fun, and you still haven't experienced the "bad grade." However, times do get hard.

Nobody really likes to talk about it here, but all of your friends that seem to be thriving are also calling their moms crying because college is hard. Adjustment is hard. When these times meet you, do not give up. Experience the emotions you are feeling, call your mom, shed a tear, and move on to the next day. I promise, it will get much better.

It is actually funny how you will connect with your best friends about how we all pretended to be okay when we actually weren't. Be willing to be vulnerable in front of them. It is amazing how close you will get, and how you will be dancing to Wannabe in your room the week before summer wishing you didn't live across the country from your new best friends.

Although vulnerability is not your strong suit, be open to new experiences. Run across campus in the pouring rain, stay up too late talking about faith, and religiously watch "Stranger Things" with a group of friends you just met. These are the experiences that you will remember when you are home over breaks and wanting to be back on campus.

I know that you are entering ND thinking that everything is perfect, but life still happens here. There are ups and downs, and the Dome can't fix all of your problems, but know that this is the place for you. ND challenges you every day to do more, be better, and make a difference. You will learn that you are in control of your destiny and that it is up to you to start making the changes that you want to see. Take advantage of the times of growth. Once you start embracing family, hope, zeal, mind, and heart, all the rest (friends, school, life, etc.) will begin to fall into place.

Enjoy every minute of this year and know that you wouldn't change a thing.

Love,

End-of-Freshman-Year Emily

Emily Graff '20
Bachelor of Science in Neuroscience
and Behavior and ACMS

Emily is native of Chicago and the first of her family to attend Notre Dame. She lived in Lewis Hall and enjoyed the beautiful views from behind the Dome and runs around the lakes. As a student, she was dedicated to Notre Dame's Women's Club Volleyball Team and served as an officer. After graduation, she intends to incorporate her interests in both neuroscience and math by participating in research.

Study what you want to study

Dear Joe,

It seems like forever since your mom and dad brought you to Notre Dame for your freshman year in August of 1972. It seems like forever because 46 years is a long time. And who would have thought in August of 1972 that I would be writing this letter 46 years later while sitting in room 343 Dillon where I live as a priest-in-residence?

What would I say to you when you were an 18-year-old boy now as a 61-year-old man?

I'm glad that you majored in what you really wanted to major in! You wanted to study Spanish and to get certified to teach high school. So, you majored in Spanish and through Saint Mary's College you were certified to teach high school Spanish. Since then you have used Spanish almost every day of your life. You taught Spanish at Little Flower Catholic High School for Girls in Philadelphia. You taught Spanish both at the University of Notre Dame and at the University of Portland. You were Pastor of two parishes—of St. John Vianney in Goodyear, Arizona, 1990-2002, and of Holy Redeemer Parish in Portland, Oregon, 2002-2009. And during those 19 years you spoke Spanish every day and celebrated Mass in Spanish thousands of times. And now for the past nine years you have worked with Latino students at Notre Dame. It would not have been possible then to imagine all the ways that God would use your ability to speak Spanish. I'm glad that you studied Spanish!

My advice: Study what *you* want to study, not what you think that you should study or what someone else tells you to study or what you think will make more money.

I'm glad that you decided to spend your sophomore year in Mexico City. That year enriched your life like no other year. You lived in a different culture, thought about a different way of life, met so many interesting and wonderful people, began to get proficient in Spanish, and so much more. Since then you have traveled to Mexico City over one hundred times. Over the years you have taken several hundred parishioners and students on trips and pilgrimages to Mexico City. You have served as a priest in a remote, almost inaccessible, village in Mexico for Holy Week and Christmas many times. All your life as a priest you have interacted with Mexican-American and Mexican people. That year in Mexico gave you a great "feel" for Mexico and her people and culture.

My advice: Study abroad. Make it fit into your major.

I'm glad that you never missed a home football game when you were a freshman. All your undergraduate years were great years of football when Ara Parseghian was the head football coach (the first three years) and then Dan Devine. We even had one national championship during your undergraduate years. Those games were so much fun. There was so much spirit, so much energy, so much life, so much love for Notre Dame!

My advice: Go to sporting events, concerts, lectures and whatever else you can. You won't regret it. In fact, you'll be greatly enriched.

I'm glad that there weren't video games in those days! You spent a lot time getting to know the guys in your section in Holy Cross Hall. You got to know almost all the guys in the hall. That was such a great hall. It broke my heart when the University demolished Holy Cross Hall in 1988. But nothing is forever—except the mercy and love of God. Some of the guys from freshman year are still close friends today. I recently baptized the grandson of one. We have a Holy Cross Hall Reunion every five years, and I try not to miss that Reunion. I also have been to several of my class reunions. I go to see friends from my college years, many of whom I made in my freshman year.

My advice: Spend less time looking at your electronic gadgets and more time talking with people.

I'm glad that we didn't have friend groups and group chats and all those other things that I don't know much about or like! Not having friend groups allowed me to meet so many interesting people. And not having group chats allowed me to talk to people, not just text them.

My advice: Make it a point to meet one or two people each semester—students or staff—whom you would not normally meet.

I'm glad that you went to Mass every Sunday of your freshman year (indeed of all your years). Though college is an important time to explore and to ask questions, I'm grateful to have remained faithful to the Faith that I was given by my parents. Notre Dame is filled with people everywhere who are willing to talk with you about your faith life and your journey with God. Notre Dame offers countless opportunities—most especially the dorm Masses every Sunday night—that can enrich and strengthen and fortify your faith. You won't make it in life without knowing the love and mercy and forgiveness of God. And it's hard for me to imagine making it without the strength given to us in the Eucharist because so much of that love and mercy and forgiveness comes to us through the Eucharist.

My advice: Go to Mass. Take advantage of the countless opportunities—religious, spiritual, academic—to come to know that you are always in the presence of God who loves you more than you can imagine.

Forty-six years is a long time. I can barely remember what I looked like. These have been great years – years of grace and mercy, of love and forgiveness. Love your freshman year. Love your freshman self. God is never absent. God is always working.

Father Joe Corpora, C.S.C.

Father Joe Corpora, C.S.C., '76, '83
Bachelor of Arts in Spanish

Fr. Joe Corpora, C.S.C., is a Holy Cross Father. Fr. Joe will be grateful to God forever for the gift of a vocation to the priesthood in the Congregation of Holy Cross. He served at the University of Portland (1983-1990), as Pastor of St. John Vianney Parish (1990-2002) in the Diocese of Phoenix, and as Pastor of Holy Redeemer Parish (2002-2009) in the Archdiocese of Portland. In 2009 he was assigned to the University of Notre Dame. Fr. Joe works in the Alliance for Catholic Education, in Campus Ministry, and with first-generation college students. He is a priest-in-residence in Dillon Hall. In December of 2015, Pope Francis appointed him to serve the Church as a Missionary of Mercy. Fr. Joe is a sinner whose sins are forgiven. And he loves anything made with tomato sauce!

With hard work, you can succeed

Dear Freshman Peter,

Believe it or not, I know how you are feeling right now. You are scared.

You are scared that you are not smart enough. Everyone at Notre Dame is a genius. Meanwhile, you are just a normal kid who got in off the waitlist as a fluke. Though it might sound strange, the fear you have right now is good. It is this fear that will give you a "chip on the shoulder" mentality. You aren't the smartest, so you're going to have to work the hardest. As a result of this fear, you are going to spend hours upon end in the library. You're going to work your tail off, and slowly but surely you are going to realize something: how you compare to your classmates doesn't matter. When you receive your first semester grades, you are going to feel tremendous pride. However, this pride does not come from comparing your GPA to your peers. Rather, it is a pride that comes from proving to yourself that with hard work, you can succeed.

You are scared that you do not have your life figured out. It seems like every other Notre Dame student knows exactly what they want to do with their life—they have their fifty-year plan mapped out. Meanwhile, you do not even know if you want to be a doctor, businessman, lawyer, or something else. To try to block out this fear, you are going to avoid it. You will absorb yourself in your studies to avoid the question of why you are studying in the first place. However, this will change. Clarity will come after a handful of meetings with the Career Center. Though you will not have your entire future figured out, you will gain something you previously lacked: excitement. Your fear of never knowing your vocation will transform into an excitement to explore your interests and passions.

So, Freshman Peter, here is my advice to you: Pray. When you are feeling scared, exercise hope by bringing that fear to God. Reflect. Take time to step back from studies and friends. Exercise mind and heart by contemplating your interests, passions, and motivations. Reach out. Step out of your comfort zone. Be courageous. Talk to new people, form friendships, and treat others with kindness. By following this advice, your fear will be replaced with feelings of fulfillment and excitement for whatever may come your way.

Sincerely,

Sophomore Peter

Peter Alexander '20
Bachelor of Business Administration in Finance

Peter Alexander is from Rochester, Minnesota, and is a member of the Class of 2020. He is majoring in finance within the Mendoza College of Business, while also pursuing a minor in Theology. Peter is a resident of Siegfried Hall and served as hall president during his freshman and sophomore years. Though he is unsure about his post-graduation plans, he has an interest in the field of investment banking.

You cannot make it alone

Dear Kendrick,

You cannot make it alone.

In high school, you were the "cross-country and track team captain, literary aficionado, trombone prodigy and honor society president" that everyone around you epitomized. You dated the "prettiest girls" and competed in the largest competitions any of your classmates had ever seen. From persevering through the trials and tribulations you experienced, you understandably believed you could handle anything single-handedly. After all, even though there is no "I" in "team," your team is hundreds of miles away in Las Vegas. Yet even without a team right there with you, I'm sure you believe confidence and intelligence will be more than enough to carry you through your academic career at Notre Dame.

You're wrong.

For as you soon may realize, the University of Notre Dame is not full of the short sighted, degrading fanatics that ostracized you from across the street in high school. This University has collected track stars, book lovers, music prodigies, and honor society students from around the world— all with unique experiences and personas that you will come to love. The only exception is that these students, who will face many of the same challenges you will, do not have to face them with an additional elective on their course load.

This elective course will in fact take many of hours of your life, keeping you awake on exam days and troubling you on weekends. It is not required for your major, nor will it help you achieve course completion in either of your double minors, but it will by far be the biggest inhibitor to success. You will need a team to help you get through it and every second you wait will hurt you in more ways than one.

For "Pretending to not be Gay" is a five-credit course and you're overloaded.

It is going to hurt, and you're going to suffer, but looking back you will finally realize how foolish you were to believe your Notre Dame friends wouldn't accept you. From the boy you hit with your trombone during the final "Band of the Fighting Irish" marching audition, to the girl who will teach you why liturgical choir music is some of the most beautiful in the world, you will form a team. This team will help you realize that a five-credit course in not being yourself is not only dumb but "high key unnecessary." You will grow strong alongside them and they will become your roommates, counselors, leaders and friends. Soon you will not only lead an organization that assists those like you, but recruit hundreds through your executive admissions role. Finally, you will stand in front of the class of 2021, your band directors and your peers and give them an induction speech of a lifetime.

You will not make it through your first year at Notre Dame alone, and I promise with the phenomenal family you meet here, you won't have to.

Kendrick

Kendrick Peterson '20
Bachelor of Arts in Political Science
with Business Economics and Public Policy

Kendrick Peterson is currently an undergraduate student from Las Vegas, Nevada, at the University of Notre Dame. In addition to living in St. Edwards Hall, he has a wide variety of commitments ranging from performing trombone in ensembles like the marching band to competing on the club cross country team. His primary major is Political Science, however with minors in Business Economics and Public Policy he definitely remains busy. In addition, he also sits as an acting officer and the Alumni outreach student representative of Prism ND (the LGBTQ+ human rights organization on campus). All of his many roles on campus have blessed him with the opportunity to truly make an impact, and hopefully over time he can become someone who encourages many others to do the same.

Never forget the time you spent at Notre Dame

Dear Regis,

My entrance to Notre Dame never would have happened if my father hadn't been in the Marine Corps and met Moose Krause in the Pacific during World War II. They became friends. (Moose played football for Knute Rockne in the 1930s, and after his service, he became the ND basketball coach for a long time). My father came home in 1945 after the war, and in 1949, I left for Notre Dame. That was 69 years ago. I left on a train from New York on a Sunday night at 6pm. The next morning, we arrived in South Bend at 6am. A bus took us to Notre Dame, and as we drove up towards the school, we saw that beautiful Golden Dome shining in the sunlight. And for the rest of your life, you knew you would never forget it. And you never did.

Notre Dame had a great football team in 1949. "Jungle Jim" Martin and Leon Hart were the guys who kept our team winning every game since 1946. Later in my life, I met both of the fellows, and it was a thrill for me to be with them and talk about Notre Dame.

But what was so great was the statue of Our Lady of Fatima—up high in the school's Grotto by the lake. The place, as you know, is absolutely beautiful. In my first year,

71

we would go there, say our prayers and feel pretty good about it when we left. Growing up in New York, I never had a chance to do that. In those days, it was just the Sunday morning Mass, but to be able to go down to that grotto at Notre Dame four times a week was something I never forgot.

The young fellows that I met in 1949 have been in my life for a long time. One of them is Dave O'Leary from Lansing, Michigan. He is a great guy, who has stayed in touch all these years, and we're still close friends.

One thing that I will always remember is a visit I made one day in my first year. It was a workout place in a small building behind the dome, and I met a priest there who had a terrific build and his name was Father B.H.B. Lange. He was tough, but he was there every day to help us out. I liked him a lot. Over the years, I've never forgotten him.

Notre Dame was a place you had to see, and you had to live there to realize how great it was. The first year was an important year for anyone who started at Notre Dame, but you had to live there to appreciate it. It was the beginning of your life, and it was the best thing that ever happened to you. I'll never forget it.

Regis

Regis Philbin '53
Bachelor of Arts in Sociology

Regis Philbin has become a cultural icon in television broadcasting and holds the Guinness World Record for the most hours on television. Regis is a TV talk and game show host, media personality, actor, author, and singer best known as the host of "Live! With Regis and Kathie Lee" and then later "Regis and Kelly." He debuted and hosted the incredibly popular "Who Wants to Be a Millionaire" game show, then "Million Dollar Password," and also "America's Got Talent." He has authored five books and has appeared on numerous late-night talk shows, sitcoms, and comedy programs. Regis graduated from the University of Notre Dame with a degree in Sociology and also served in the US Navy. Regis and his wife, Joy, enjoy dividing their time between New York City, Connecticut, and Los Angeles.

Give up trying to know everything

Dear Christian,

I know that you are having a tough time adjusting to college. Don't worry. God clothes the grass of the field. Anyways, this year is going to fly by. You are going to mess up, but you manage to bounce back. We are alive, and one might even say that we are thriving. Classes are no joke, but you are prepared. There are a couple of insights that I should share with you.

Firstly, there is definitely time to go to daily Mass. It won't seem like it for a while, but that is OK. You will make it to that realization when you need it most. Also, taking time to pray every day feels great. You are almost always going to be distracted, but don't stop trying.

Next, you really need to try to remember people's names. There are so many Michaels and Matthews. Remembering names will help you know people in the dorm better. Otherwise, it becomes embarrassing. It isn't the end of the world when you can't remember many though. It will come along.

Also, it is important to realize right now that you will not have enough time to exercise like you used to do. Just go for shorter workouts when possible. Sleeping is so important, but this will cut into time for other things. Try not to cut out friends though. They are hard to come by.

I have something important to say, but I am going to be purposefully vague: trust in your gut. It just may be God trying to help you out. He will be there for you when pretty much everyone else is gone. Don't worry so much about people that don't actually care about you. Love your friends and family. Call Rogelio or PJ. Talk with Erica.

Finally, give up trying to know everything. You have a great support system, and you do not have to stand on your own to make people proud of you. At the end of the day, God is your all. The people around you are His presence in your life. Maybe we don't know what we are doing, but maybe that's OK. Really, stop trying and just listen. Silence is hard to find, but seek God there.

Love,

You

P.S. Quick tips: Friendsy is a trap. Stache Bash will happen. Boxing will hurt.

Christian Dennis '20
Bachelor of Science in Civil Engineering
Christian Dennis is a Civil Engineering major scheduled to graduate in Spring 2020. He is a member of the Liturgical Choir, Compass Leadership, and Right to Life. He is a townie from the great city of Mishawaka, Indiana with Mom, Dad, and two younger sisters right down the road. He could not feel more blessed than to be at the University of Notre Dame accompanied by his Notre Dame family.

Don't settle for a pedestrian life

Dear Kenn,

Let me start by saying welcome to Notre Dame. You wanted so badly to come here ever since that first time you visited. You knew it wouldn't be easy, not only because of the high admissions standards (remember you had to have at least 1200 on the SAT's or it was nearly impossible to get admitted) but also because I know you are wondering "how am I going to afford the $2,800 tuition plus room and board of $1,100?" Certainly, you won't have much money to drink beer, even though the drinking age is 18 in Michigan and you can jump on the University shuttle bus that leaves every 30 minutes from the circle to Kubiak's bar on the weekends!!!

Now, not everyone at Notre Dame will be this position, but don't feel less because of it, and don't ever fall into the trap of measuring the size of the person by the size of their wallet.

And, let me assure you, you will be able to afford Notre Dame and you should view this as one of the many challenges that you will experience in your life. I know this is hard to understand because right now you are digesting the fact that many things have migrated from your parents' responsibility to yours. See, up to now, your parents have provided most everything including support, guidance and security. But, one of the purposes of college is to introduce you to anxiety, challenges and conflict. (It's one of the reasons you no longer have your own private bedroom.) I know it's different and surprising, but embrace the challenge. View it as any other class you have at Notre Dame. It is the chance to learn and to grow. Don't add more stress and anxiety to yourself by worrying about stress and anxiety. Don't retreat to your parents when the going gets tough. Always task yourself with resolving conflicts, dealing with the anxiety and accepting the challenges on your own or with the help of your peers. Becoming competent at these skills will be handy in everything you do in life because, from now on, life will require this of you. Also, there is nothing like the reward that comes from surmounting these issues. You will become confident, empowered, optimistic and enthusiastic. What better skills would you want when you leave Notre Dame?

You are going to have the opportunity to meet the University's President, Father Hesburgh. You won't think much of it at first but spend as much time with him as you can. You will many times look back on his words and actions for inspiration and guidance. When he tells you that the key to a successful life is to:

1. Be true to your God
2. Be as good as your parents
3. And, champion the causes of underdogs— write it down and repeat it to others as often as possible.

When you die, you get to take two things with you — who you love and what you know. There is no better place than Notre Dame to begin filling up these two categories. So, make the time and effort to cultivate lifelong relationships and—it goes without saying at an educational institution—learn as much as you can.

Now is the time to broaden your horizon. Learn to seek out opinions and positions with which you may not agree. Learn to disagree in a respectful way. Always leave others their dignity. Try as many different things and different subjects as possible, even if you think they are outside your comfort zone. Challenge your own thoughts and goals.

Make sure when you leave Notre Dame that you find what you are passionate about. Find the one thing that excites, motivates and inspires you. What you are passionate about can't be what someone else wants you to do because at the end of the day, you cannot live someones else's life, you have to live *your* life!!

You can't find your passion on the internet, you can't Google it. It's not on Facebook . . . (wait a minute, you don't even know what I am talking about!) Just remember, your passion comes from your heart. Use your time at Notre Dame to learn what's in your heart. Now, it is not enough to merely find your passion . . . you must incorporate a component of service to others in what you do. And, there is no better place than Notre Dame to find opportunities to hone your skills at learning to be of service to others. So, along the way, learn the importance of friendship, community, empathy, compassion and service to others.

When you leave Notre Dame, marry the passion you find in your heart with the compassion you have learned from your family and from your time at Notre Dame. Spend your life being passionate about what you do and compassionate about how you do it.

Don't settle for a pedestrian experience at Notre Dame or a pedestrian life!

Also—and this is important—ditch the platform shoes, madras shirts and the patchwork bell bottom jeans. I know you think you are cool, but you are going to feel so silly when your kids see the pictures of you in them!!

By the way, buy as many stocks as you can in May of 1982 when the Dow Jones industrial average will be at 2,100 pts.... You will be shocked at what happens!!

Finally, time is precious. Make the most of it, so fly privately whenever you can!!

Kenn

Kenn Ricci '78
Bachelor of Business Administration
Degree in Accountancy

Kenn is a 38-year aviation industry veteran beginning in 1980 with Corporate Wings, an aircraft charter operation. Today, he is the principal of Directional Aviation Capital which owns a glomerate of aviation companies including Flexjet, Sentient Jet, Sky Jet, Nextant Aerospace, Stonebriar Commercial Finance and Constant Aviation. Kenn was honored as an Ernst & Young Entrepreneur of the Year and received the Harvard Business School's Dively Entrepreneurship Award. He was the youngest recipient of the prestigious William Ong Award for extraordinary achievement in the general aviation industry and was recently honored as a "Living Legend of Aviation." He serves on the Notre Dame Board of Trustees and Kenn and his wife Pamela announced the first ever $100 million gift to the University. His management strategies have been featured in the Wall Street Journal, and he is the author of Management by Trust, a book featuring practical management techniques for building employee trust and success.

Be open to the music life brings

Dear Theresa,

As I write this, I am listening to the Palestrina playlist, which has grown considerably in the past nine months. It seems fitting to begin with music, since your year will both begin and end with music. To be more precise, your year will begin with disappointment—but I promise you, not making Folk Choir will open doors for blessings you can't begin to imagine.

The song has shifted to Josquin's *Salve Regina*, a style of music you never realized you would enjoy. Most of your year, in fact, will be beyond what you imagined. You're beginning college knowing that you love Theology and are excited about PLS, but you will discover an authentic joy in your classes and confirm every part of your hope for this education. I know you have high standards for yourself (which will be confirmed first semester), but don't let chasing a GPA keep you from enjoying the courses contributing to it.

The playlist has shuffled to Josquin's *Ave Maria*—do you remember singing that at St. Matt's? It's a beautiful thing to have memories and connection to home, but be careful to allow yourself room to grow. Don't be afraid to call home and ask Dad to pick you up to spend time with Mary, but don't allow the obligation of seeing family pressure you into spreading yourself too thin. This song is beautiful because it's so familiar to you; but the unfamiliarity of a new piece is also important because it teaches you openness. This openness doesn't have to mean saying yes to everything, and choosing to say no doesn't mean you'll never get another opportunity.

The song changed to "Lo He Comes," which will always make you think of Daniel. It'll be a tough year for goodbyes for you: Christian, Daniel, Meg, WLC. Trust me that it will be okay, and that those tears aren't always going to be frustrated or sad. They'll be tears of laughter at Gaven's inability to be serious, or tears of joy as you gaze around the choir loft and fall in love with music yet again. They'll be tears from being too exhausted to breathe, and those tears will be the most beautiful of all, because you'll get to cry in that PW chapel which you feel so uncertain about right now. It becomes one of your favorite places on campus, and a stage for the small miracles of life.

I thought about letting the final song shuffle, but instead I chose "I Was Glad." You're still going to struggle with decisions, so I wanted to assure you that while it's okay not to have an idea of where you want to end up, it's also good to make intentional choices. Tell those new friends you want to spend time with them. Invite yourself along when a group goes on a walk on tour. Text Erica and get dinner with her. Have a real conversation with Tommy, or Georgi, or Kaelyn. Take a walk around the lakes alone; eat with an acquaintance at the dining hall and make a friend.

I am so excited for you. You are going to love Lit Choir,

and PW, and Queen Week, and Catherine's bridal shower, and meeting Matthew for the first time, and those exhausting Saturdays in the fall. You are already a wonderful young woman, and I am so proud of your growth.

A final warning—you might even start to like coffee! Best of luck and many prayers,

Theresa

Theresa Rice '20

Bachelor of Arts in the Program
of Liberal Studies and Theology

As a native of South Bend, Notre Dame has always been part of the background for Theresa's life. The fifth of her six siblings to attend Notre Dame, she studies PLS and Theology with the vague idea of teaching after graduation. She is a passionate member of both Liturgical Choir and Women's Liturgical Choir, spending hours each week in CoMo or the Basilica rehearsing music which has come to shape her time at ND. When she's not singing, she can usually be found in Pasquerilla West Hall, anywhere with free coffee, or walking around campus wishing for a warmer coat.

Welcome home

To my freshman year self,

Welcome home! You are about to embark on a four-year journey that will forever change your life. You may not realize this now, but after four years it will be hard to imagine that you ever thought of going anywhere else.

Notre Dame is a really amazing place, as you're about to find out. You may feel scared and a little alone right now—know that you're not the only one feeling like this. This feeling will seem crazy to you in four years when you're crying with your friends on graduation night, wondering where the time went and wishing you could do it all over again. When that day comes (and it's going to come faster than you think!), make sure you have no regrets. Notre Dame has so much to give you, so take every little thing that you can.

Before you left for college, Mom shared some life advice with you. She said, "Only half of what you will learn in college will be in the classroom." Don't forget this. You're about to spend four years surrounded by some of the smartest and most hardworking people in the country. It's easy to feel as if you should spend every waking moment studying, especially during those times when you're really struggling and wondering if you're actually smart enough to be here. Remember to take a step back and appreciate your life and the people in it. Is staying up with your friends talking until

3 a.m. when you should be doing your homework a good choice? Well, you may be a little tired the next day, but I promise you—you will still pass that class, and it's not the nights you spent studying alone that you're going to remember in 10 years. Your professors have so much to teach you, but don't discount the lessons that you'll learn from other people in your life—whether it's a mentor, your best friend, or someone in front of you in the Starbucks line.

The words "Welcome home!" may seem like a cheesy line that someone in the Admissions Office came up with to recruit students. You walk into your dorm room on move-in day, greeted by an extremely enthusiastic Welcome Weekend staff, and meet your new roommate for the first time. You make your way through your first week of classes, wondering how you're going to possibly have time to finish your homework. You cheer in the stands on Game Day, eat lunch in the dining hall, take a few trips to the Grotto. And slowly but surely, you start to realize that Notre Dame is more than just a school. You finally understand what everyone means when they call it home.

Before you know it, you'll be hugging your friends on graduation night, wondering how you will possibly live without these people that have become your family in this place you now call home. So, don't blink, and make sure to enjoy every second.

Alyson

Alyson Duzansky '17
Bachelor of Science in Chemical Engineering
Alyson Duzansky is a Class of 2017 graduate. She graduated with a degree in Chemical Engineering and was an active member of the Society of Women Engineers. She is currently living in Washington, D.C. and working for Accenture as a Technology Consultant.